Heroes in the Flames

by Kate Fisher
illustrated by Eric Velasquez

Chapters

Harcourt

Orlando   Boston   Dallas   Chicago   San Diego

Visit *The Learning Site!*

www.harcourtschool.com

Firefighters

Firefighters play an important role in all communities. Fighting fires is a dangerous job. Firefighters often risk their own lives to save others.

Fires can happen at any time, so firefighters must be prepared, day or night. In rural areas, firefighters are often volunteers. They must be prepared to leave their jobs, family activities, or beds whenever they hear the siren. They go to the fire station, get their firefighting gear, jump aboard a fire truck, and head to the fire.

In larger towns and cities with full-time, paid firefighters, the firefighters take turns working at the fire station around the clock. A firefighter will usually be on duty for three days in a row, day and night.

The Fire Station

The fire station is divided into several areas. The largest area is the engine room, where the fire trucks are kept. The trucks are always parked facing the street. This is a good policy because it means the trucks can be driven out of the station quickly. No time will be wasted when a call for help comes in.

The special clothes that firefighters wear are kept in a room near the engine room. This allows firefighters to grab them quickly on their way out. To save time, they put on their gear in the trucks, on the way to the fire.

Each fire station has a special room called a watch room. This is where the phones and alarms are kept. Normal policy requires that someone stay in the watch room at all times to receive calls.

Many fire stations are two stories tall. The kitchen, eating area, and bunk room are often located on the second level. Two-story stations have a pole leading down to the first level. That's because it's faster and safer to slide down the pole than to run down the stairs.

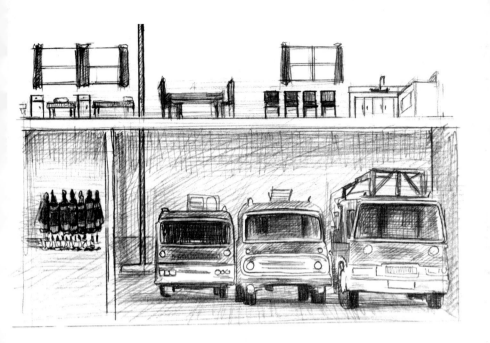

Firefighters prepare their own meals in the kitchen and eat them in the dining room. If supplies have dwindled, they might go shopping for food. If they must leave the station, they always take their two-way radios with them, so they can be called in case of an emergency.

Each station has a bunk room, where the firefighters sleep. It might not be as comfortable as home, but it is comfortable enough for the firefighters to get a good night's sleep.

Fire stations also have training areas. Firefighters can exercise here by lifting weights and doing other types of training. Often, they practice firefighting methods here. As practice, they might go up and down ladders carrying dummies that weigh as much as a grown person.

Anyone who has ever veered from an exercise program knows that it is easy to get out of shape, but firefighters must stay in good shape. Their job takes a great deal of strength. Training and exercise are part of their regular routine.

Fire Trucks

There are many kinds of fire trucks. Each is used for a different purpose. The pumper, or fire engine, carries water, long hoses, ladders, rescue equipment, and a pump. The pump, which forces water out through the hoses, is the most important part of this truck.

Another kind of fire truck carries the tower ladder. This ladder carries firefighters to the top of very tall buildings.

Yet another kind of truck carries an aerial ladder, which is used for rescuing people. This kind of truck doesn't carry water or hoses.

The rescue unit carries extra equipment that might be needed at the scene. A special kind of truck called the foam unit carries foam instead of water. This truck is used to put out chemical and oil fires at places such as factories, airports, and highways.

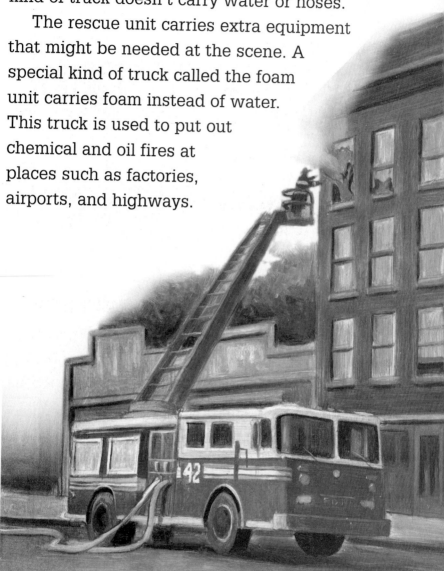

Fire!

When a call comes in, the firefighters stop whatever they are doing and rush into action. They check with the watch room to find out where the fire is. The station alarm will ring for about thirty seconds. By the time it stops, the fire engines are already on the way to the fire.

The firefighters kick off their shoes before they get into the truck. Once in the fire engine, they start putting on their gear. They put on their fireproof scarves and hard hats. Then they pull on their heavy rubber boots and waterproof pants.

Next, they put on special coats called turnout coats. These coats are also waterproof. The turnout coats are lined inside with a special cloth that helps keep the firefighters cool while they are near the heat of a fire.

The last thing the firefighters put on is their breathing apparatus, which is stored in the truck. This helps the firefighters breathe when the air is full of thick smoke.

On the way to the fire, the firefighters look at maps that tell them where the nearest fire hydrants are. When they get to the fire, the pumper's driver unwinds a hose and attaches it to a hydrant. The hydrant leads to water pipes underground, where there is plenty of water to fight the fire.

The driver then opens the hydrant, using a wrench. This allows water to flow into the pumper. From there, it is forced out through another hose that is aimed at the fire.

It takes several firefighters to hold the hose. The person who is in front, near the nozzle, has the hardest job. That person can usually hold the nozzle for only a few minutes.

The pressure of the water coming out is very strong, almost like a geyser, and makes it difficult to control the hose. As soon as the strength of the person in front has dwindled, he or she signals for relief. Then the next person takes over. Controlling the stream of water coming from the hose takes a lot of strength. The firefighters have to take turns at this difficult job.

A fire needs heat, fuel, and air to keep
burning. By hosing water onto the flames, the
firefighters cool down the flames and keep air
from getting to them. This works with most fires.
However, water can make oil and chemical fires
spread. That's why firefighters spray
thick foam or powder on these types
of fires to smother them.

Even when a fire seems to be out, the
firefighters' job is not over. Embers that are still
hot can get the fire started again. It only takes a
little tinder to fuel a fire. The firefighters must
make sure that all embers are put out
completely, so they can't ignite any more tinder.

Forest fires are treated differently from other kinds of fires. They are so big that it's impossible to get enough water to put them out. Once the treetop canopy is ignited, the fire can spread quickly. The wind can whip the flames from one tree to another until the fire seems to be out of control.

The way firefighters deal with forest fires is to cut down trees that are ahead of the spreading fire. Then they use tools to dig out trenches around the fire. When the fire gets to the treeless, grassless trench, there is no fuel to burn, so the fire can go no farther.

A Proud Tradition

Firefighters are proud of the work they do. They must be very brave and willing to spend time away from their families. They also must work hard to stay in good shape, so they will have the strength to do their job well. These are not the most important parts of their job, however. Often, they must risk their lives to save other people from fires. For their courage, they are often honored at special ceremonies. People should be grateful for the work that firefighters do to protect their community.